Catato and Friends

CATATO. The first Plantanimal—
part cat and part potato.

Poems and Illustrations
by Renie B. Adams

A Catato and Friends™ Book
www.CatatoAndFriends.com

Text and illustrations © 2012 Renie B. Adams
www.RenieBee.com

Published by Little Chickadee Media
1505 Castlerock Dr., Fort Collins, CO 80521
info@littlechickadeemedia.com
www.LittleChickadeeMedia.com

ISBN: 978-0-578-10168-2
Library of Congress Control Number: 2012934720

Signature Book Printing, Inc.
www.sbpbooks.com
First Printing, March 2012
Printed in USA

To David

"David," an embroidery by Renie

Professor Peach's CATATO

"Let's create a Plantanimal breed.

A mix of parts is what we'll need.

Examine this oddball I call a 'CATATO'—

Look! He's part cat and part a potato!

A splendid example—to me so it seems—

The first Plantanimal born in my dreams."

Freddy's Doubt

Professor Peach, the children's teacher,

Inspired them with her curious creature.

"For homework this week, you'll each create

Your own Plantanimal! Won't that be great?

And remember," she said to skeptical Fred,

"Anything's possible in your own head."

Pat's APRICAT and HIPPOTATO

"I'm giving CATATO a couple of cousins—
An acrobatic APRICAT
And a HIPPOTATO who juggles hats.
We'll all gather by the dozens
To see their awesome act," said Pat.
"Can't you just imagine that?"

Benny's RUTABEAGLE

Benny's baby beagle Ada

Chased and caught a rutabaga.

Ada was a naughty pup—

She ate the rutabaga up!

Then she became a RUTABEAGLE,

And that made Benny have to giggle.

Freddy's Mixed Feelings

Freddy stopped at Ben's for a while,

And, in spite of himself, he had to smile.

"Make believe is dopey really,

Yet I guess I have to confess—

RUTABEAGLE, though certainly silly,

Is still a great success!"

Russell's BRUSSELS TROUT

"Oh, dear," wondered Russell, "I really wish
I could make a Plantanimal out of a fish."
Troubled by doubt, his face in a pout,
He thought it would NEVER work out.
Then—suddenly—he heard himself shout,
"HOW ABOUT A **BRUSSELS TROUT!**"

Peggy's PIGGLES

When Peggy jiggled her piggy bank,
Out popped two dimes and a nickel—
"Quite enough money to buy me a pickle!"
Tickled pink, she thanked her bank,
Then had a hunch that made her giggle,
"A pig plus a pickle adds up to a PIGGLE!"

Freddy's Decision

Freddy puzzled, "How did Peg think of PIGGLES?
They're not real, but I'd like them to be.
I'd take a pet PIGGLE home with me—
OK! I'll make up my own Plantanimal!
I'll try **very hard** to think of one
That's **really real** and lots of fun."

Mary's RASPBEAR and BLUEBEAR

A berry is a sweet little fruit,

But a bear is big and scary.

"Could I mix these two?" mused Mary.

"A RASPBEAR would be very cute!

But I truly love the color blue—

So I'd love a wee BLUEBEAR, too."

Peter's BUMBLEPEAS

Peter wouldn't eat his peas.

His puppy wouldn't either.

Mama said, "Peter, please!

No sweets until those peas are gone!"

So he wished that they were BUMBLEPEAS

And prayed that they would fly from home!

Helen's OTTERMELON

Helen watched her otter, Walter,

Flop in the river and float in the sun.

"His tummy's so round and plump," said Helen,

"I could turn it into a watermelon.

Painting it green would really be fun,

And Walter would be an OTTERMELON."

Paul's COWWIFLOWER

Paul lived on a farm and helped his pop
Care for the cow and the cauliflower crop.
"Cow—cauli—cowwi—caul,"
Paul turned the words all around.
"Wow, what about a COWWIFLOWER?
I've got to jot that down!"

Freddy's Worry

"I'm very worried," Fred said to Paul.
"So far I've thought of nothing at all!"
"Don't be worried," Paul said to Freddy.
"You're just not totally ready.
A Plantanimal will come to you."
COWWIFLOWER agreed and said, "Moo."

Artie's ARTICHICK

An artichoke leaf looks like a wing,

Which made Artie think about birds.

What idea would his thinking bring?

He started to play with some words.

Witty Artie, very quick,

Changed "-choke" and hatched an "ARTI-CHICK"!

Nina's LLAMA BEAN

Nina's mama served her lunch—
Lima bean soup and banana punch.
"Look at this lima bean," Nina said.
"It's got four legs, a tail, and a head.
I believe it's turned into a LLAMA BEAN—
The silliest thing I've ever seen!"

Freddy's Regret

Fred wished **he'd** thought of a LLAMA BEAN.
He wished he could think of anything!
Parsnips? Foxes? Mangos? Prunes?
Bats? Broccoli? Crabs? Raccoons?
"I think I just can't think," thought Fred.
"**Nothing's** possible in **my** head!"

Freddy's FLAMANGO

Fred finally stopped thinking and rested instead,

And two fancy FLAMANGOS popped into his head!!

He happily watched as they danced a fandango—

His heaven-sent mix of flamingos and mangos!!

His sister, Sally, who saw his show,

Teased, "Sorry, Freddy, but **I** don't think so!"

CATATO'S Friends

All the Plantanimals met at school
And found each other uncommonly cool.
Each one so different, yet plain to see
They belonged to a special family.
All the children were thrilled at the sight,
And Professor Peach swooned with delight!

"Bugs," an embroidered self-portrait

About the Author

Renie Breskin Adams is a professor of art,
retired from Northern Illinois University in DeKalb.
Her works in fiber arts have been exhibited internationally,
and her narrative embroideries are in major public collections,
including the Renwick Gallery of the Smithsonian Institution
in Washington, D.C. and the Museum of Fine Arts Boston.

In recent years, Renie has become addicted to making
art in her computer. All of the poems and illustrations
in Catato and Friends were created there.
This is her first children's book.

**Visit Renie's gallery and blog at
www.reniebee.com.**